Financial Crimes Enforcement Network

The Role of Domestic Shell Companies in Financial Crime and Money Laundering:

Limited Liability Companies

November 2006

Department of the Treasury
Financial Crimes Enforcement Network

The Role of Domestic Shell Companies in Financial Crime and Money Laundering: Limited Liability Companies

---

> ▶ **Executive Summary and Key Findings**

By virtue of the ease of formation and the absence of ownership disclosure requirements, shell companies – generally defined as business entities without active business or significant assets – are an attractive vehicle for those seeking to launder money or conduct illicit activity. While business entities generally, and shell companies specifically, have legitimate commercial uses, this lack of transparency in the formation process poses vulnerabilities both domestically and internationally.

The advantages of using these business entities for legitimate business purposes are in some senses outweighed by the potential for abuse presented by some entities, and by the risks to and potential deleterious effects on the financial system that result from lack of transparency regarding beneficial ownership.

Although the focus of this paper is on limited liability companies, other business entities, including trusts, business trusts, and corporations, are also vulnerable to abuse. The intent is to demonstrate the nature of the vulnerabilities that limited liability companies present, provide examples of known abuses, and present some specific steps which can be taken to reduce the risk to the financial system while preserving the advantages of limited liability companies for legitimate business use.

It is anticipated that attention will be given in the future to studying other business entities which are subject to abuse and illicit use as shell companies or to otherwise mask ownership for illicit purposes.

This report does not attempt to address tax policy issues regarding shell companies. The vulnerabilities addressed are those that relate to the use of shell companies to facilitate money laundering and financial crime in general.

Key findings

The following key findings demonstrate the vulnerability of shell companies to misuse, and the imperative to formulate appropriate responses to address the issue.

- Domestic shell companies (LLCs and other varieties) have some legitimate and legal uses, but the ability to abuse such vehicles for illicit activity must be continually monitored.

- Domestic shell companies can be and have been used as vehicles for common financial crime schemes such as credit card bust outs, purchasing fraud, and fraudulent loans.

- The use of domestic shell companies as parties in international wire transfers allows for the movement of billions of dollars internationally by unknown beneficial owners. This could facilitate money laundering or terrorist financing.

- Company formation agents and similar service providers play a central role in the creation and ongoing maintenance and support of domestic shell companies, some of which appear to be used for illicit purposes domestically and abroad.

- Based on our research, states do not appear to impose effective accountability safeguards on company formation agents and similar service providers to ensure that the business entities they create, buy, sell, and support are not violating state laws specifying that the companies be used only for lawful and allowable purposes.[1]

- There is currently no requirement that these service providers report suspicious activity involving the shell companies they have created, bought, sold, or supported, nor are there requirements or procedures to identify beneficial owners in certain jurisdictions if illicit activity is suspected.

- Certain domestic jurisdictions, especially when serviced by corrupt or unwitting service providers, are particularly appealing for the creation of shell companies to be used for illicit purposes.

- The LLC, particularly when organized in a state which does not require reporting of information on ownership,[2] provides an attractive vehicle for a shell company because it can be owned or managed anonymously and is inherently vulnerable to abuse.

Steps Forward

FinCEN is undertaking three key initiatives to deal with the issues addressed in this report and to mitigate risks posed by shell companies:

1. Concurrent with this report, FinCEN is issuing an advisory to financial institutions highlighting indicators of money laundering and other financial crime involving shell companies, and reminding financial institutions of the importance of identifying, assessing, and managing potential risks associated with providing financial services to such entities.

2. FinCEN is continuing its outreach efforts and communication with state governments and trade groups for corporate service providers to discuss identified vulnerabilities, and to explore ways to address vulnerabilities in the state incorporation process, particularly with respect to the lack of public disclosure and transparency regarding beneficial ownership of shell companies and similar entities.

3. FinCEN is continuing to collect information and studying how best to address the role of certain businesses specializing in the formation of business entities in its effort to reduce money laundering and related vulnerabilities in the financial system through the promotion of greater transparency.

---

[1] A few states – most notably Delaware — impose "standards of conduct" on persons serving as "registered agents." For example, the Court of Chancery in Delaware can enjoin a person from serving as a "registered agent" if the person has engaged in criminal conduct or in conduct that is likely to deceive or defraud the public. Service as a "registered agent" forms only part of the services that company formation agents and similar service providers often offer their clients. Moreover, a business entity need not organize or conduct activities in Delaware or any other state that imposes "standards of conduct."

[2] Although some states require the reporting of information on ownership, no state requires the reporting of information on beneficial ownership. An individual may own an LLC indirectly, through nominees and other business entities. The Securities and Exchange Commission (SEC) addresses the potential through the concept of beneficial ownership, which the SEC defines as holding the rights of ownership "directly or indirectly, through any contract, arrangement, understanding, relationship, or otherwise." The concept of beneficial ownership would require an LLC – when reporting information – to "look through" nominees and business entities.

The term "shell company" generally refers to limited liability companies and other business entities with no significant assets or ongoing business activities. Shell companies – formed for both legitimate and illicit purposes – typically have no physical presence other than a mailing address, employ no one, and produce little to no independent economic value. Shell companies are often formed by individuals and businesses to conduct legitimate transactions, such as domestic and cross-border currency and asset transfers, or to facilitate corporate mergers and reorganizations.

Shell companies can be publicly traded or privately held. Although publicly traded shell companies can be used for illicit purposes, the vulnerability of the shell company is greatly compounded when it is privately held and beneficial ownership can more easily be obscured or hidden. Lack of transparency of beneficial ownership can be a desirable characteristic for some legitimate uses of shell companies, but it is also a serious vulnerability that can make some shell companies ideal vehicles for money laundering and other illicit financial activity.

One of the common uses for a shell company is in the *reverse acquisition*.[3] The procedure will often involve a simple acquisition of a shell company, with shares of a private company used as consideration. The shell company, which at one point may have been an active company publicly traded on a stock exchange, issues shares to the shareholders of a private company sufficient to give those shareholders a majority interest in the shell company, thereby effectively taking the private company public without the usual costs associated with an initial public offering, and giving shareholders of the private company control over the shell company. It should be noted that the shell company in the reverse acquisition is often a formerly active company, not one created solely to be a shell.

The reverse acquisition process has in the past been subject to abuse. For example, if the expected value of the private company is fraudulently exaggerated, investors buying into the company may lose a considerable percentage of their investments when the company turns out to be worth much less. Those who fraudulently promoted the company have at that point already sold their stock and made a handsome profit. These "pump and dump" schemes often involve shell companies with low market capitalization whose stock trades at pennies per share on the "pink sheets" (www.pinksheets.com), OTC Bulletin Board, or other over-the-counter trading and information systems. One indicator of this scheme is concentrated trading in normally thinly traded stocks. Ralph A. Lambiase, former president of the North American Securities Administrators Association (NASAA) and director of the Connecticut Division of Securities, noted in 2004 the existence of "a steady stream of fraud and misconduct in the distribution and manipulation of shares of shell companies and the companies that combine with shell companies."[4]

Some steps have been taken to prevent this type of abuse. For example, the SEC adopted rules on June 29, 2005 designed to protect investors in the

Shell Company Domestic Abuses

Pump and dump	Over invoicing
Credit card bust out	False invoicing
Fraud	

securities markets from fraud and abuse involving the use of shell companies, while allowing the use of shell companies for legitimate corporate structuring purposes.[5] The SEC's rules are disclosure-oriented

---

[3] Also known as a *reverse merger or takeover*.

[4] "NASAA Wants All Merged Shell Companies to Provide Full Disclosure, Transparency," *M2 Financial Wire*, 06/28/2004.
[5] SEC Release Nos. 33-8587; 34-52038; International Series Release No. 1293; File No. S7-19-04, "Use of Form S-8, Form 8-K, and Form 20-F By Shell Companies," 70 FR 42233 (July 15, 2005).

and require the public reporting of information that would then be accessible through the Electronic Data Gathering, Analysis, and Retrieval system (EDGAR). The SEC acknowledged in its rulemaking that companies and their professional advisors often use shell companies for many legitimate corporate structuring purposes, such as certain change of domicile or business combination transactions.

Shell companies may play a role in common financial crime schemes such as the credit card bust-out, whereby credit is built up on cards using false identities, then phony transactions with cooperating businesses or shell companies are made and the phony charges are received as payments from the unsuspecting credit card companies. Referring to a case involving a foreign national who is suspected of providing bust-out proceeds to terror groups, FBI Intelligence Analyst Joseph Enright said, "one of the co-conspirators in the bust-out case linked to the New York case had an American identity under one name, with which he incorporated shell businesses and obtained checking accounts, and a completely different 'new name' under which he obtained a passport from his native country."[6] Additionally, the complicit businesses may change names, director names, and addresses on official documents to throw investigators off the track.

A technique commonly seen by corporate accountants involves an employee over-invoicing or creating false invoices and pocketing the difference. The director of a nutritional supplement company was convicted of money laundering in 2004. He had set up a shell company and was paying false invoices for the purchase of nutritional supplements. In addition, he received kickback payments from another nutritional supplement company in exchange for purchasing their products. His company was established by a service provider that also provided mail and phone forwarding for the shell company.[7]

The latter example indicates that the individuals or companies that create shell companies may play a significant role even after the shell is created and sold. In fact, a convenient and popular service combines formation with ongoing support.

One Delaware-based service provider provides formation services as well as mail forwarding

services, telephone lines, e-mail accounts, and accounting services to file tax returns. A number of suspected shell companies created by this firm appear in Suspicious Activity Reports.

Forming and supporting small companies is neither difficult nor expensive, and requires no special skill other than understanding the laws in the various states. The majority of shell companies sold to foreign interests appear to differ significantly from those used in reverse acquisitions, for example, in that they appear to have been set up solely for purchase and were not "aged" or put on the shelf after some period of actual operation (though they, too, may not be used immediately). This type of shell appears to have few legitimate uses, and can fairly easily be employed to disguise ownership or movement of assets or to facilitate illicit activity.

A report by the U.S. General Accounting Office (now the Government Accountability Office) in 2000 provided information on another service provider whose business provided approximately 2,000 shell companies to clients based in Moscow, Russia. The report did not uncover the purpose of these companies, but did describe some interesting aspects of a phenomenon that appears to be continuing today on a large scale – the use of domestic shell companies to hide the ownership and purpose of billions of dollars in international wire transfers. This phenomenon has been drawing increasing attention both domestically and abroad due to the large amounts of money involved and the secretive nature of the companies and their transactions. The Financial Crimes Enforcement Network has previously examined the use of domestic shell companies in these transactions and has provided input to the Financial Action Task Force (FATF).

▶ Advertised Services for Shell Companies

Internet searches reveal that numerous service providers advertise services for shell companies, such as resident agent and mail forwarding services. Shell companies may also purchase corporate office service packages in order to establish a more significant local presence. Advertised prices for these packages, which often include a state business license, a local street address and an office that is staffed during business hours, a local telephone listing with a live receptionist, and 24-hour

[6] "Are bust-out schemes financing terror?," *Vision*, FBI New York, 04/07/2005.

[7] "Information issued by U.S. Attorney's Office for the Northern District of Texas on March 11: Former director of sports nutrition at Texas Tech University sentenced to 33 months in federal prison," *US Fed News*, 03/11/2005.

personalized voicemail, range from $900 to $1950 per year in the research sampling. In addition, service providers may offer assistance in opening local and foreign bank accounts for the shell company. For example, in the GAO report cited earlier, it was revealed that two service providers created 236 accounts at two U.S. banks which were the recipients of about $1.4 billion in wire transfers.

Service providers may also sell aged "shelf companies." Prices for these companies vary depending on the year and state of organization (older companies commanding higher prices), as well as factors such as whether the shelf company has an employee identification number (EIN), received a Paydex score, filed non-activity tax returns, previously had a bank account, or currently maintains a bank account. Advertisements by some service providers contend that the main advantage for purchasing a shelf company is to provide the appearance of longevity to the business, particularly for the purpose of meeting minimum age requirements when obtaining leases, credit, and bank loans.

In order to preserve a client's anonymity, some service providers promote a variety of nominee services including:

- **Nominee EIN**: Shell companies may obtain an EIN without providing the client's EIN on the application.

- **Nominee officers and directors**: Service providers may set up nominees for those offices in the shell company that appear on the public record in order to eliminate the client's name from secretary of state records. In addition, a client can retain ownership and operational control through confidential stock ownership or appointment to offices that do not appear on the public record (*e.g.*, vice president).

- **Nominee stockholders**: The client may use nominee stockholders to create an additional layer of privacy while maintaining control through an irrevocable proxy agreement.

- **Nominee bank signatory**: A nominee appointed as the company accountant accepts instructions from the client.

▶ Limited Liability Companies

Though there are other types of business entity available, a very common type formed and operated as a shell company is the limited liability company (LLC). In fact, the LLC makes an attractive vehicle for a shell company. Some LLCs can be owned or managed anonymously, and are therefore inherently vulnerable to abuse. Virtually anyone can own or manage an LLC, including foreign persons and other business entities. A *member* of an LLC is equivalent to a shareholder in a corporation. A *manager*, on the other hand, is equivalent to an executive officer or a member of the board of directors. An LLC may lack managers, in which case the members would manage the LLC. Some states do not require the names or addresses of members or managers. In some cases, only the names of managers and not members (owners) are reported.

According to the International Association of Commercial Administrators (IACA), an organization that solicits annual reporting from the states, of the states reporting, there were more than 4.9 million LLCs active or in good standing at the end of 2005 (See Figure 1).[8]

---

[8] Referenced figures and tables are located at the end of the report.

LLCs

Limited liability companies first became widely available in the U.S. in the early 1990s. The German version (GmbH, or *Gesellschaft mit beschränkter Haftung*) has been in existence since the late 1800s. The LLC is a hybrid form of business entity that can protect the owners effectively in the case of legal action. Like a corporation the LLC structure removes the members and managers from liability, and, like a partnership, it provides certain tax benefits. It is considered a "pass-through" arrangement because the individuals are taxed rather than the company (unless the company elects to be taxed as a corporation.). An LLC is easier to set up than a corporation and LLCs are subject to relatively few procedural requirements relating to the governance of the business entity.

As reported to IACA, the following five states had the most LLCs active or in good standing in 2005 (AK, IN, NM, PA, and WY did not report this statistic):

State	LLCs Active or in Good Standing (2005)
Delaware	333,565
California	325,738
Florida	293,845
New York	275,503
Michigan	274,940

Out of 35 states reporting (Michigan and Florida, among others, did not report this statistic), the top five states for revenue collected from LLC initial filings in 2005 were:

State	Revenue Collected in 2005 (initial filings)
Illinois	$13,639,250
Texas	$12,021,100
New York	$11,281,600
Delaware	$8,779,200
Massachusetts	$7,184,000

California was ninth with $4,901,680 collected. See Figure 2 for an example from Nevada of the various

fees which contribute to the revenue generated by LLCs.

Illinois reported 138,256 LLCs active or in good standing in 2005. All of the above figures include both domestic and foreign LLCs. States use the term *domestic* to refer to business entities formed in their state. A *foreign* business entity is considered one formed in a state or jurisdiction other than the one to which it is applying for registration. A foreign LLC must file with the state in order to "do business" in that state. It is important to understand that companies owned by out-of-state or foreign persons or entities are formed as domestic LLCs unless they were originally formed in another jurisdiction. Therefore, newly created shell companies owned by such persons or entities will often fall into the domestic classification.

Reporting to IACA shows an increase for most states in the number of new LLC filings in the last five years (see Figure 3), with Florida posting the greatest percentage increase – 410.67% – from 2001 to 2005. Pennsylvania is next with 215.08%. For 2005, IACA reports show that Florida was the leader for new domestic LLCs (123,437 compared to the next highest by Delaware at 87,360) and the leader in total LLCs formed between 2001 and 2005 – 357,239. California was the leader in registration of foreign LLCs in 2005 (10,593 reported, compared to the next highest by Florida at 7,121).

▶ The Vulnerability of Certain States based on their Laws

Figures 4 through 8 illustrate the trends in LLC formation in four states – Delaware, Nevada, Oregon, and Wyoming – that are representative of those that have formation and reporting requirements which may be attractive to those persons seeking to hide illicit activity within the framework of shell companies. It is important to note that these same requirements also attract legitimate business activity. A comparative discussion of the formation of limited liability companies in these and other states follows.

▶ Limited Liability Company Requirements

Limited liability companies in Delaware, Nevada, Oregon, and Wyoming may be formed by one or more persons. See Table 1 for a comparison of the four states' initial formation requirements and fees. The certificate of formation required to form LLCs in these states must include the name of the LLC and the name and address of the registered agent and registered office. See Figure 9, Delaware's Certificate of Formation, for an example.

A critical element in the formation of a shell company to be used for illicit purposes is the lack of transparency regarding ownership. States whose laws do not require LLCs to report the identities of members or managers will be most attractive to persons seeking to form a shell company for illicit purposes. (However, even a requirement to identify a member or manager can be thwarted through the use of nominees or fictitious identities.)

The categories that follow are based on degrees of transparency assigned on the basis of FinCEN's preliminary understanding of each state's reporting requirements. The states in the first category offer the least transparency. All limited liability companies organized or "doing business" in a state must file one or more of the following documents – articles or a certificate of formation or organization, periodic reports, and an application for registration as a foreign entity. We have placed states in categories based on whether a limited liability company must report information in at least one of these documents. In addition, we have placed states in categories based on whether the limited liability company must report information on at least one person – and not all of them. To illustrate, if a state requires a limited liability company to report in a certificate of formation the identity of only one member and only one manager – and requires reporting of the information in no other document -- then the state will have been placed in the last category.

The statutes of a few states include language requiring the execution or signing of a document by a person whose identity the limited liability company need not report in the body of the document itself. For example, a statute may impose no requirement to report the identities of either members or managers. The statute may nevertheless indicate that "a member

or manager must sign documents filed with the Secretary of State." Since the language is intended to ensure that the filing of a document is duly authorized – and not to ensure that the limited liability company includes information on members or managers – the language has no effect on the category in which the state would fall.

Fourteen states impose no requirement to report the identities of either members or managers. These states are listed below:

Arkansas	Mississippi
Colorado	Missouri
Delaware	New York
Indiana	Ohio
Iowa	Oklahoma
Maryland	Pennsylvania
Michigan	Virginia

Eight states and the District of Columbia require a limited liability company to report the identities of managers only. These jurisdictions do not require a limited liability company to report the identities of members, even when the limited liability company has no managers:

Massachusetts	Tennessee
North Carolina	Vermont
Rhode Island	Wisconsin
South Carolina	District of Columbia
South Dakota	

Twenty-four states require a limited liability company to report the identities of members, but only when the limited liability company lacks managers. These states are listed below:

California	Nebraska
Connecticut	Nevada
Florida	New Hampshire
Georgia	New Jersey
Hawaii	New Mexico
Idaho	North Dakota
Illinois	Oregon
Kentucky	Texas
Louisiana	Utah
Maine	Washington
Minnesota	West Virginia
Montana	Wyoming

The following four states are the only ones that require a limited liability company to report the identities of members regardless of the existence or number of managers:

Alabama	Arizona
Alaska	Kansas

Therefore, 47 jurisdictions in the U.S. exist in which ownership of an LLC may legally remain unreported, depending on how the LLC is structured. (And, as noted above, the conclusion does not address the potential for concealing identity through the use of nominees or similar mechanisms.)

The 14 states that impose no requirement to report the identities of either members or managers provide the least transparency. The following table identifies their ranking in terms of number of new LLCs formed in 2005 and the percentage increase (if available) from 2001 to 2005 according to reporting to IACA (also see Figure 3):

States with Lesser Transparency	Rank (of 47 reporting): New LLCs - 2005	% Increase in New LLCs 2001-2005
Delaware	2	102.13%
New York	5	111.87%
Michigan	8	86.28%
Colorado	9	133.37%
Ohio	11	92.77%
Virginia	13	136.08%
Maryland	15	106.81%
Missouri	16	N/A
Pennsylvania	19	215.08%
Oklahoma	30	N/A
Mississippi	32	N/A
Arkansas	35	107.29%
Iowa	37	109.20%
Indiana	N/A	N/A

Similarly, taking the average increase for each of the four groups of states yields the following comparison:

Comparison of states	
Level of Transparency (Least to Most)	% Increase in New LLCs 2001-2005
No Reporting of Managers or Members	120.09%
Reporting of Managers Only	112.00%
Reporting of Members When an LLC Lacks Managers	146.68%
Reporting of Managers and Members	138.75%
Average of all states reporting:	133.37%

- The average increase in new LLCs from 2001 to 2005 for the states with the least transparency was 120.09%.

- The states that provide the next level of transparency averaged a 112.00% increase from 2001 to 2005.

- The states that require information on members only when an LLC lacks managers had an average increase of 146.68%.

- The four states that provide the greatest level of transparency averaged an increase of 138.75%.

- The average increase in number of LLCs (2001-2005) for all states reporting to IACA was 133.37%.

In terms of percentage increase in new LLC filings there appears to be no definitive correlation between level of transparency and preference of a state for LLC formation. States with more transparency have exhibited slightly higher growth on average than states with less transparency, but there is much variation within each category. Other factors appear to account for the relative popularity of certain states over others.

Of the four states which are often recognized as being particularly appealing for the formation of shell companies (Oregon, Wyoming, Nevada, and Delaware)[9], only Delaware falls in the group offering the least transparency. The other three states fall in the group offering a moderate level of transparency.

A preliminary conclusion based on the above information suggests that having all states require LLCs to report the identities of members and managers would not significantly affect the number of LLCs formed or the relative balance among states. Therefore, it appears that the vulnerabilities of the states which provide less transparency could be reduced through requiring greater transparency without a major effect on revenue generated for those states. In contrast, the ensuing benefits to law enforcement and regulatory entities of greater transparency could prove significant.

---

[9] See, e.g., Money Laundering Threat Assessment Working Group, "U.S. Money Laundering Threat Assessment," (Dec. 2005) at pp.47-50; U.S. Government Accountability Office Report No. GAO-06-376 to the Permanent Subcommittee on Investigations, U.S. Senate, "Company Formations: Minimal Ownership Information is Collected and Available" (April 2006).

Abuse of LLCs

The LLC can be used as a vehicle or tool in a wide range of illicit activity. The potential lack of transparency and ease of formation could make it useful for money laundering and other financial crime. Examples include:

Becs International LLC was a key company in a high profile case which broke in 1999 involving Russian money moved through the Bank of New York and a large network of shell companies.

Capital Consultants, LLC was at the center of an elaborate scheme to defraud benefit plan investors of hundreds of millions of dollars. Investigations started in 1993 and ended with the indictment of 11 individuals, seven of whom pled guilty and one of whom was convicted in a bench trial. Several shell companies were involved, including **Sterling Capital LLC**, **Brooks Financial LLC**, and **Beacon Financial LLC**. In a statement given to the Senate on June 9, 2005, Alan D. Lebowitz, Deputy Assistant Secretary for the Department of Labor's Employee Benefit Security Administration (EBSA) said, "The scheme was of great sophistication and had a veneer of respectability provided by the cooperation of so many professionals including attorneys, accountants, and investment advisors. EBSA's investigation uncovered a complex scheme to defraud investors through the unprecedented use of newly created shell companies, paper transactions, and false reports."

A lawyer in Oregon was sentenced to prison in February 2004 and forced to pay restitution of more than $400,000 for engineering several fraudulent loan schemes. He used a shell company to help defraud five different financial institutions.

availability. For illicit purposes, the services and advice of particular service providers may be another key factor.

There are additional issues concerning business activity conducted by LLC shells. While a shell company by definition has little or no assets, it may act as a conduit for the transfer of funds between third parties and members of the company. There are no requirements that the company report activity as a conduit. Many states do not consider the LLC to be "doing business" in the state simply because it maintains an account at a bank in that state. In that case, the LLC need not be registered with the state as a foreign business entity if it is not otherwise active there. Similarly, many states consider "isolated transactions" as falling outside the definition of "doing business" in the state. Therefore, an LLC conducting isolated transactions as a conduit may have no obligation to register as a foreign business entity. The LLC could organize in a state offering the least transparency and conduct activities in a number of other states without reporting the identities of members or managers.

There are additional ways to further obscure ownership and activity. For example, because an LLC can be owned or managed by one or more other business entities – a corporation, a limited partnership, a general partnership, a trust, or even another LLC – layers of ownership can be devised which make it highly unlikely that relations between various individuals and companies can be discerned, even if one or more of the beneficial owners are actually known or discovered. In Delaware and other states, an LLC serving as a member or manager for another LLC is not considered to be "doing business" in the state solely by reason of being a member or manager of the other LLC. An LLC serving as member or manager of another LLC could organize in a state offering the least transparency and conduct activities in a number of other states without reporting the identities of members or managers.

An additional benefit that applies equally to LLCs (or corporations) formed in any state is the air of legitimacy afforded foreign owners in operating a U.S.-based company. Further legitimacy may possibly be obtained by organizing in a state without an international reputation for privacy of ownership.

Again, other factors may be at work in determining the preference of one state over another for the organization of a shell company. These might include considerations of convenience as well as

► Suspicious Activity Reporting

Research in the FinCEN Financial Database found 1,002 Suspicious Activity Reports (SARs) filed from 1996 through the beginning of 2005 which identify activity that appears to be related to shell companies. This is a sampling which almost certainly does not contain all of the SARs related to domestic shell company activity. The filing institution may not recognize the involvement of shell companies or may not indicate its suspicions clearly in the SAR. Preliminary analysis of SARs filed since this research was conducted indicates that financial institutions continue to file SARs on shell company activity. Much of the increase in the last several years may be attributable to heightened awareness of shell company "red flags" (see *The SAR Activity Review*, Issue 7, Aug. 2004, p. 7) as well as to agreements entered into by several major banks with their primary federal or state bank regulators to address deficiencies relating to compliance with applicable federal and state anti-money laundering laws, rules, and regulations.

These SARs reveal a wide variety of domestic and offshore financial center activity. Suspected shell company locations include the United States, the Cook Islands, Vanuatu, Bahamas, the United Kingdom, Panama, the Cayman Islands, Nigeria, and Antigua. 932 SARs identify activity involving suspected U.S.-based shell companies. 67 SARs identify activity primarily involving shell companies in typical offshore financial centers with some connection to a U.S. entity or financial institution. (38 of these SARs identify suspected shell banks in foreign locations such as Uruguay, the Cook Islands, St. Lucia, and St. Vincent/Grenadines.) The activities or location of the suspected shell companies in the SARs have some nexus with the United States. Because the SAR filers frequently do not or cannot provide information regarding the location of suspected shell companies (business location, mailing address, address of registered agent), the actual number of U.S.-based shell companies cannot be accurately determined. Many of the SARs identify multiple companies as possible shell companies.

Of the SARs describing recent domestic shell company activity in the United States, there are examples of a suspected Ponzi scheme, pump-and-dump stock fraud, telephone "cramming" by organized crime, possible money laundering by

politically exposed persons, and various other suspected frauds and suspicious movements of money, particularly through wire transfers.

Foreign Abuse of U.S. Shell Companies

A review of SAR data on both a macro and micro scale indicates that suspected shell companies incorporated or organized in the United States have moved billions of dollars globally from accounts at banks in foreign countries, particularly those of the former Soviet Union, and predominantly the Russian Federation and Latvia. Most of these companies are LLCs and corporations.

Many of the U.S.-based suspected shell companies were observed to maintain banking relationships with Eastern European financial institutions, particularly in Russia and Latvia. Of the 1,002 SARs identified, 768 involved suspicious international wire transfer activity involving domestic shell companies which follow certain recurring patterns and share common characteristics. These SARs identify what appear to be 1,361 different suspect individuals and business entities, including 329 U.S.-based LLCs, as SAR suspects.[10] In addition, 504 of the SARs identify Russia and 449 identify Latvia as locations of activity in the narrative portion. See Figure 10 for a breakdown of countries frequently associated with activity in these SARs. The aggregate suspected violation amount reported by these SARs is nearly $18 billion.[11]

In contrast to the SARs identifying domestic or typical offshore center activity, these 768 SARs provide even less information on suspects owing to the lack of information provided in wire transfer communications and the anonymity provided by the use of shell companies.

The wire transfers described in many of these SARs originated at accounts in Russia or Latvia held by

---

[10] The number of truly unique subjects is probably slightly less due to alternate spellings, misspellings, incomplete identification, etc.
[11] As with the other SARs in this sampling, the actual total is somewhat less.

what appear to be U.S. shell companies, passed through the correspondent accounts of major U.S. banks or branches of foreign banks, usually in New York, and then were sent back overseas, often to a wide variety of beneficiaries in many locations. There are many variations of this basic flow. See Figure 11 for a model of the typical flow of funds in this pattern. Reporting of such activity has increased considerably since 1999 – see Figure 12.

Because this type of SAR is only filed if a U.S.-based bank or branch is involved in the wire transfer chain, it is conceivable that banks outside of the United States may be handling similar activity that is not being reported through the U.S. system.

The following elements of suspicious activity in these SARs are cited repeatedly:

- Insufficient or no information available to positively identify originators or beneficiaries of wire transfers (using Internet, commercial database searches, or direct inquiries to a correspondent bank). The lack of identifying information on the transactors is one of the most frequently cited concerns

- U.S. company with Latvian or Russian bank account in U.S. dollars formed in U.S. state that does not require the reporting of information on ownership

- Foreign correspondent bank exceeds its client profile for wire transfers in a given time period or individual company exhibits unusually high amount of activity, sometimes in bursts inconsistent with normal business patterns

- Payments have no stated purpose, do not reference goods or services, or identify only a contract or invoice number

- Goods or services, if identified, do not match profile of company provided by correspondent bank or character of the financial activity; companies reference remarkably dissimilar goods and services in related wire transfers (for example, computers, footwear, steel, meat products, dairy products, sporting goods, lids, auto parts, film extruders, sugar, coolers, pet resins, tissue, furs, mining machinery, maintenance and support, tutoring, marketing); explanation given by foreign

correspondent bank is inconsistent with observed wire activity

- Transacting businesses share the same address, provide only a registered agent's address, or other address inconsistencies

- Many or all of the wires are sent in large, round dollar, hundred dollar, or thousand dollar amounts

- Unusually large number and variety of beneficiaries receiving wires from one company

- Frequent involvement of high-risk offshore financial centers, especially as location of beneficiaries; sometimes many jurisdictions involved

- Use of nested correspondent banking situations in Russia or Latvia[12]

- Repeated SAR filings on same suspects (i.e., ongoing activity over a period of months)

Many additional suspect entities (business entities and individuals) are identified by name in the SAR narratives, which often contain what limited originator, beneficiary, and wire reference information may be available to the U.S.-based bank filing the SAR. Because in most cases the filing bank is simply a middle link in the wire transfer chain, there is little information on the originator and beneficiary entities – often just a company name with no other identifying information. Definitive identification of shell companies solely from wire transfer records is therefore rarely possible.

The owners of the companies involved in these transactions are very difficult or impossible to identify. However, it is possible that some identification may be made by correspondent banks, though this information is often considered by the filing institution to be insufficient proof that the transactions are legitimate.

The combination of correspondent banking and domestic shell companies provides an opportunity for foreign or domestic entities or individuals to move money via wire transfers or other methods without disclosing their true identities or the nature or

---

[12] "Nesting" refers to the use of a foreign bank's correspondent account with a U.S. bank by another foreign bank to gain access to the U.S. banking system.

purpose of the transactions. In effect, the domestic shell company could be a vehicle to launder money, move money derived from crime, or finance terrorist activities and groups, all completely anonymously. SAR information indicates that some U.S. banks have closed their correspondent accounts with foreign banks which did not provide adequate identification of the wire transactors or purpose of the wires.

Requests from Foreign FIUs

Case data suggests that foreign Financial Intelligence Units (FIUs) have an interest in U.S. companies that may be shells. For example, through the first half of 2005, 15% of research requests made to FinCEN from the Latvian FIU, 21% from the Bulgarian FIU, 25% from the Slovakian FIU, 33% from the Russian FIU, and 55% from the Ukrainian FIU identified an LLC as the primary subject.

Because of the lack of ownership information for these companies, U.S. banks holding correspondent accounts for foreign banks will have difficulty corroborating the foreign banks' claims that the foreign correspondent banks know their customers. In addition, law enforcement often is forced to investigate these companies through requests to Financial Intelligence Units (FIUs) in the appropriate countries. Despite these companies being formed in the United States, successful identification and research sometimes may be possible only through requests for investigative efforts overseas.

Various reports provide a further indication of the level of foreign concern about the abuse of U.S. shell companies. A lawsuit filed in Delaware's Chancery Court alleges that the Russian Izmailova "mafia" laundered millions of dollars through U.S. shell companies.[13] The *Wall Street Journal* reported that law enforcement agencies in Russia and 13 other countries made more than 100 requests to obtain subpoenas on Delaware companies in a four-year period ending in September 2004.[14]

A possible solution which tackles the problem at its root is to examine the laws and requirements which prevent law enforcement and regulatory authorities from conducting effective investigations into the ownership of business entities. Such steps as requiring company formation agents and similar service providers to obtain and maintain records of beneficial ownership for the companies they service could be considered. The information could then be made available at the request of government authorities under appropriate circumstances. In addition, greater transparency in reporting requirements under state law could reduce the value of business entities as vehicles for illicit activity.

▶ Steps Forward

FinCEN is undertaking three key initiatives, set forth below, to deal with the issues addressed in this report and to mitigate risks posed by shell companies..

1. **Issue an advisory to alert financial institutions maintaining accounts for domestic non-publicly traded business entities about the particular risks associated with domestic shell companies.**

To assist U.S. financial institutions in identifying and mitigating potential risks associated with accounts maintained for shell companies, FinCEN is issuing, concurrent with this report, an advisory that highlights some indicators of money laundering and other financial crime involving such entities.

The advisory provides an overview of shell companies and agent and nominee service providers, describe some of the vulnerabilities posed by these business entities and service providers, describes indicators of money laundering, highlights published reports concerning shell companies, and outlines how to manage the risks of providing services to shell companies by reference to the provisions of the Business Entities (Domestic and Foreign) section of the FFIEC BSA/AML Examination Manual, dated July 28, 2006.[15]

---

[13] "Is Russian mob exploiting Del. law?; Chancery Court lawsuit claims criminals are using 'corporate veil' to launder money," *The News Journal* (Wilmington, DE), 11/26/2004.
[14] "Laundering queries focus on Delaware," *Wall Street Journal*, 09/30/2004.

[15] http://www.ffiec.gov/pdf/bsa_aml_examination_manual2006.pdf.

2. **Conduct outreach to state governments and appropriate trade groups.**

FinCEN continues its outreach to financial institutions, state governments and appropriate trade groups to explore ways to address vulnerabilities in the state incorporation process, particularly with respect to the lack of public disclosure and transparency regarding beneficial ownership of shell companies and similar entities. Positive experiences with Delaware on the issue of bearer shares lead us to believe that some states could be motivated to take prompt steps to remedy weaknesses in their statutory schemes. Other states may be less willing to take those steps.

3. **Continue to study what role certain businesses specializing in the formation of business entities may play in addressing existing vulnerabilities.**

FinCEN is continuing to collect information and studying how best to address the role of certain businesses specializing in the formation of business entities in its effort to reduce money laundering and related vulnerabilities in the financial system through the promotion of greater transparency.

Given their role in forming and supporting business entities, these service providers – which could include attorneys, trustees, and other intermediaries specializing in the business of providing services relating to the formation and support of business entities – are in a unique position to know and obtain information about beneficial owners, to determine whether these entities are to be used illicitly, and to recognize suspicious activity. They have information that can be critical to law enforcement, regulatory authorities, and other financial institutions in combating the use of shell companies to promote illicit finance. Moreover, they are in the best position – in the first instance – to discourage abuses by reducing the ability of the beneficial owners of these entities to operate anonymously (and, consequently, with relative impunity).

Figure 1

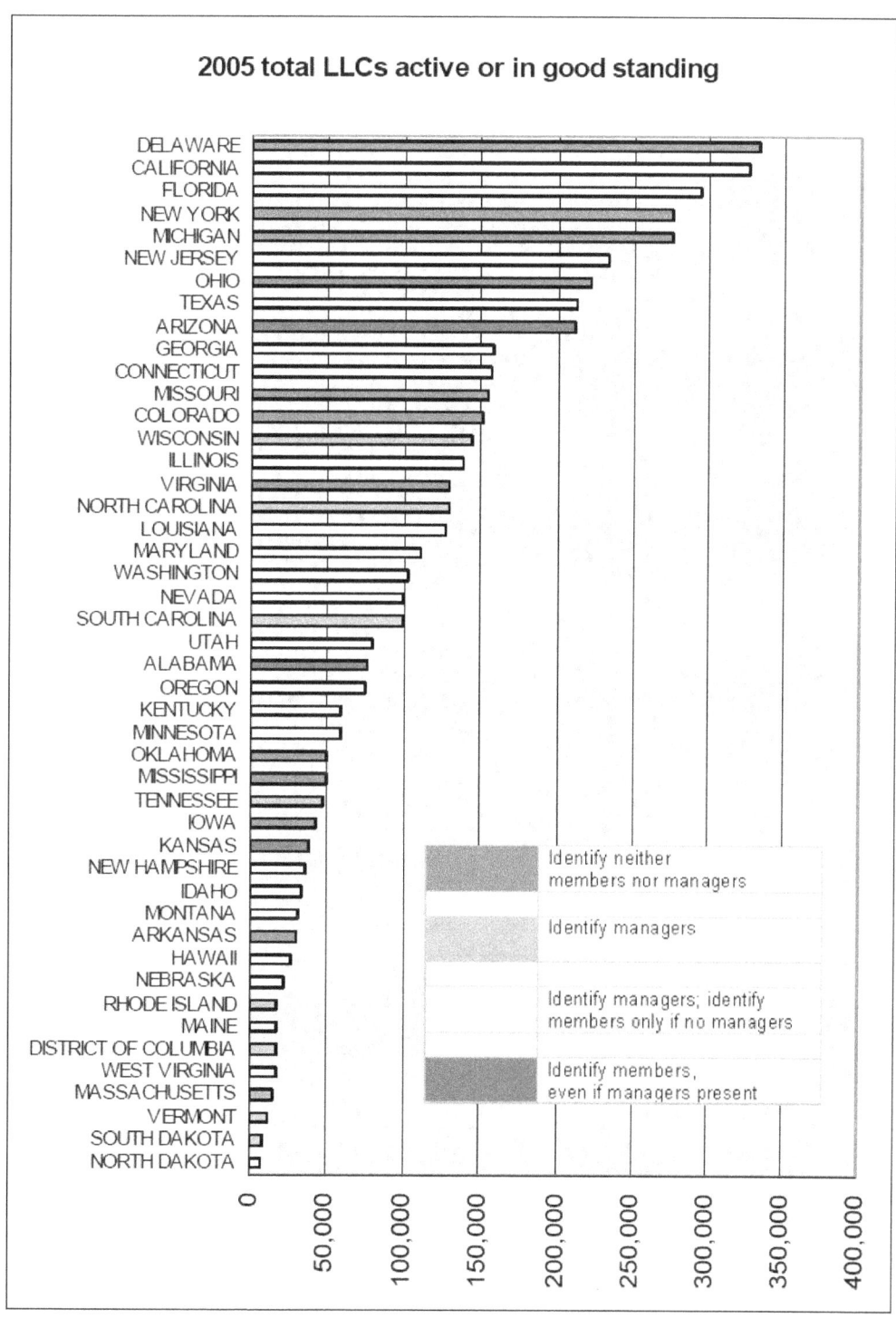

Source of data: International Association of Commercial Administrators (IACA), Annual Report of the Jurisdictions, 2006. AK, IN, NM, PA, and WY did not report this statistic.

Figure 2

DEAN HELLER
Secretary of State
202 North Carson Street
Carson City, Nevada 89701-4201
Phone: (775) 684 5708
Website: secretaryofstate.biz

```
Limited-Liability Company
Fee Schedule
Effective 10-1-05
```

LIMITED-LIABILITY COMPANY FEES: Pursuant to NRS 86 for both Domestic and Foreign Limited-Liability Companies.

Articles of Organization	$75.00
Registration of Foreign Limited-Liability Company	$75.00
Reinstatement Fee	$300.00
Certificate of Amendment	$175.00
Restated Articles	$175.00
Certificate of Correction	$175.00
Certificate of Termination (pursuant to NRS 86.226)	$175.00
Merger	$350.00
Termination Pursuant to NRS 92A	$350.00
Dissolution of Domestic Limited-Liability Company	$75.00
Dissolution of Foreign Limited-Liability Company	$75.00
Preclearance of any Document	$125.00
Articles of Conversion – contact office for fee information	
Articles of Domestication – contact office for fee information	
Revival of Limited-Liability Company – contact office for fee information	
24-Hour Expedite fee for above filings	**$125.00**
Change of Resident Agent/Address	$60.00
Resident Agent Name Change	$100.00
Resignation of Manager or Managing Member	$75.00
Resignation of Resident Agent (plus $1.00 for each additional entity listed)	$100.00
Name Reservation	$25.00
24-Hour Expedite fee for above filings	**$25.00**
Apostille	$20.00
Certificate of Good Standing	$50.00
Initial List of Managers or Members	$125.00
Annual or Amended List of Managers or Members	$125.00
24-Hour Expedite fee for above filings	**$75.00**
Certification of Documents – per certification	$30.00
Copies – per page	$2.00
Late Fee for List of Managers or Members	$75.00

2-Hour Expedite is available on all of the above filings at the fee of $500.00 per item.

1-Hour Expedite is available on all of the above filings at the fee of $1000.00 per item.

PLEASE NOTE: the expedite fee is in addition to the standard filing fee charged on each filing and/or order.

<u>24-HOUR EXPEDITE TIME CONSTRAINTS:</u>

Each filing submitted receives same day filing date and may be picked up within 24 hours. Filings to be mailed the next business day if received by 2:00 pm of receipt date and no later than the 2nd business day if received after 2:00 pm. Expedite period begins when filing or service request is received in this office in fileable form. The Secretary of State reserves the right to extend the expedite period in times of extreme volume, staff shortages, or equipment malfunction. These extensions are few and will rarely extend more than a few hours.

Nevada Secretary of State Form Fee Schedule-LLC 2003
Revised on: 09/26/05

Figure 3

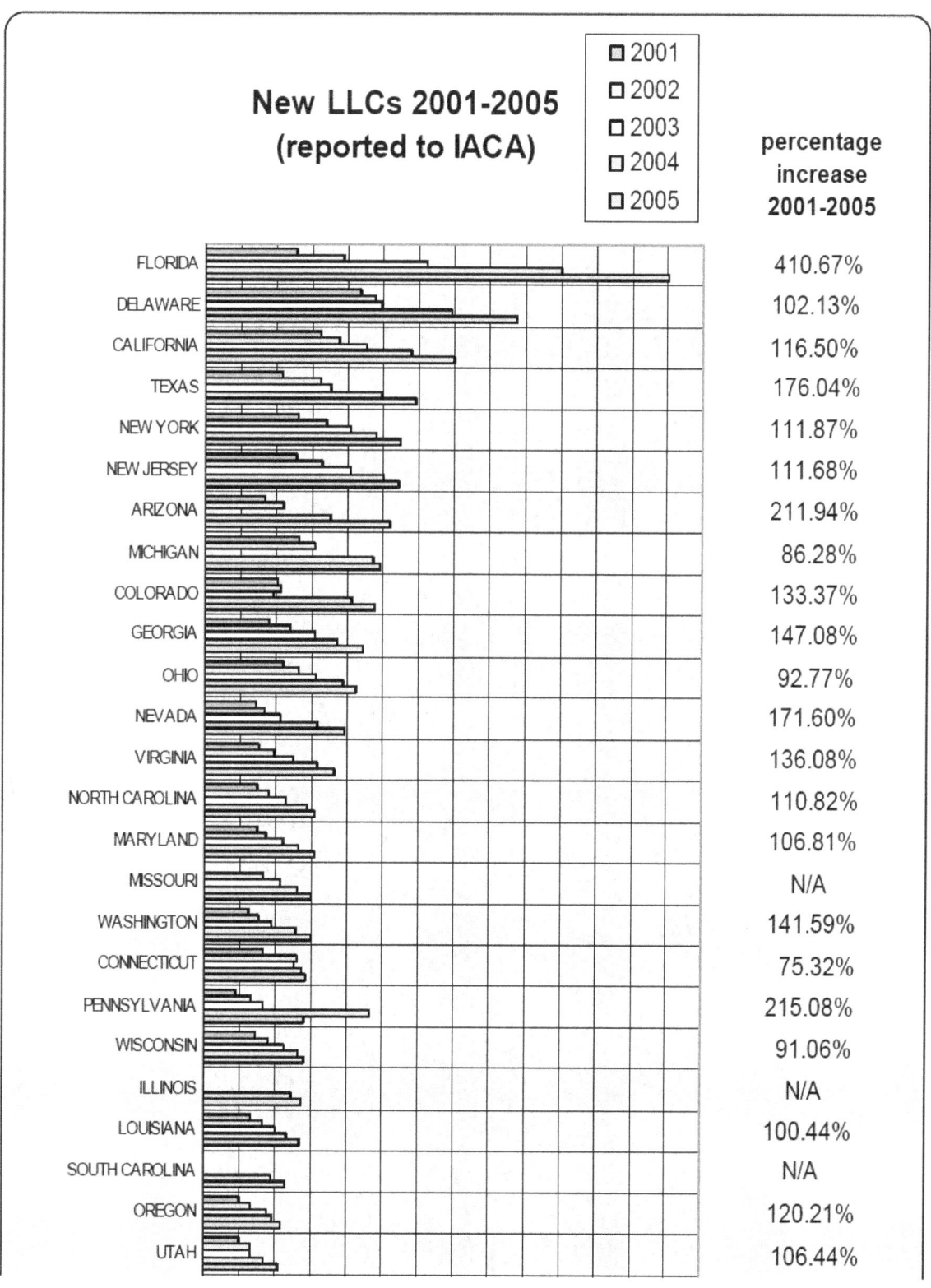

New LLCs 2001-2005 (reported to IACA)

	percentage increase 2001-2005
2001	
2002	
2003	
2004	
2005	

State	percentage increase 2001-2005
FLORIDA	410.67%
DELAWARE	102.13%
CALIFORNIA	116.50%
TEXAS	176.04%
NEW YORK	111.87%
NEW JERSEY	111.68%
ARIZONA	211.94%
MICHIGAN	86.28%
COLORADO	133.37%
GEORGIA	147.08%
OHIO	92.77%
NEVADA	171.60%
VIRGINIA	136.08%
NORTH CAROLINA	110.82%
MARYLAND	106.81%
MISSOURI	N/A
WASHINGTON	141.59%
CONNECTICUT	75.32%
PENNSYLVANIA	215.08%
WISCONSIN	91.06%
ILLINOIS	N/A
LOUISIANA	100.44%
SOUTH CAROLINA	N/A
OREGON	120.21%
UTAH	106.44%

(Continued next page)

(Continued)

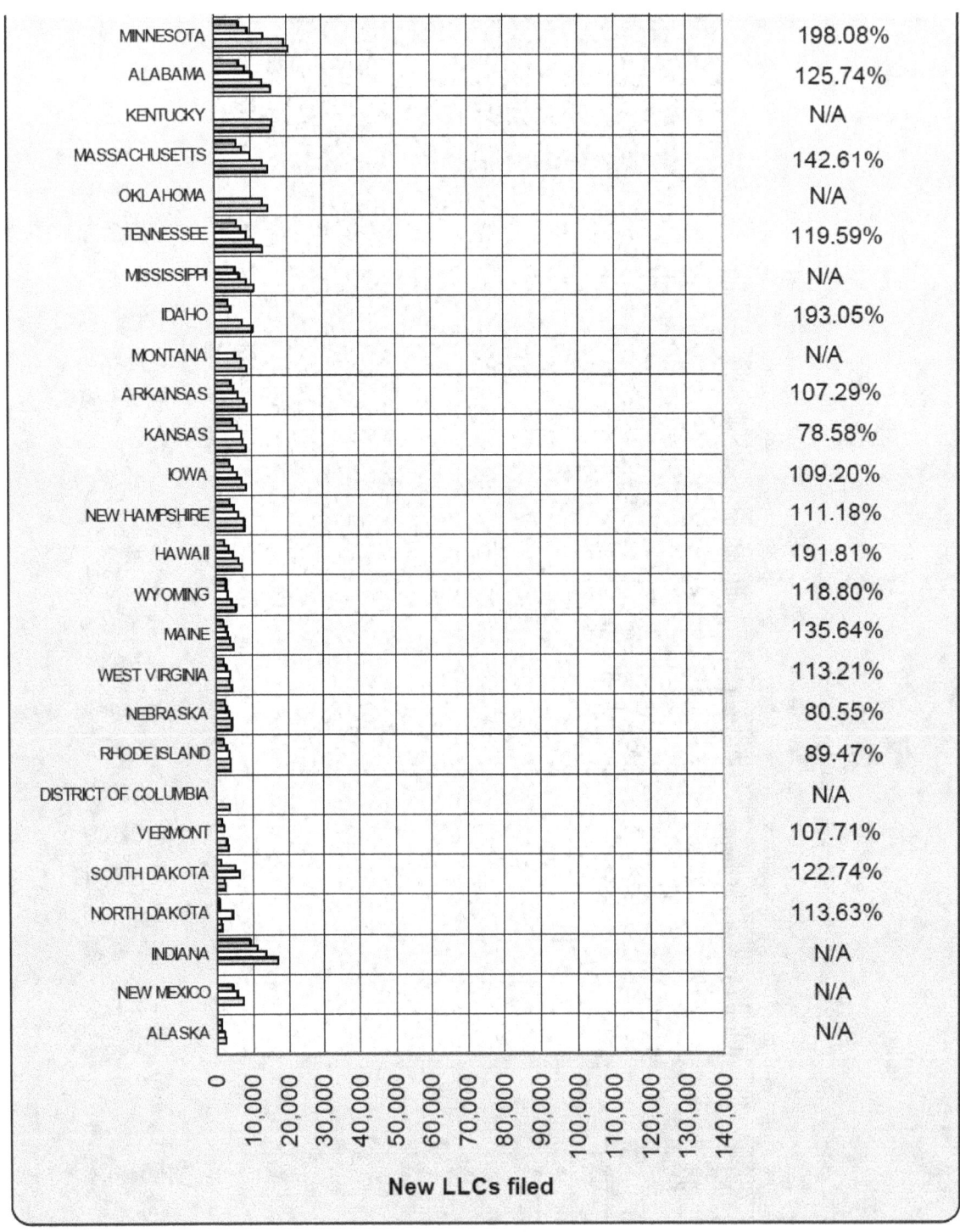

State	New LLCs filed	Percentage
MINNESOTA		198.08%
ALABAMA		125.74%
KENTUCKY		N/A
MASSACHUSETTS		142.61%
OKLAHOMA		N/A
TENNESSEE		119.59%
MISSISSIPPI		N/A
IDAHO		193.05%
MONTANA		N/A
ARKANSAS		107.29%
KANSAS		78.58%
IOWA		109.20%
NEW HAMPSHIRE		111.18%
HAWAII		191.81%
WYOMING		118.80%
MAINE		135.64%
WEST VIRGINIA		113.21%
NEBRASKA		80.55%
RHODE ISLAND		89.47%
DISTRICT OF COLUMBIA		N/A
VERMONT		107.71%
SOUTH DAKOTA		122.74%
NORTH DAKOTA		113.63%
INDIANA		N/A
NEW MEXICO		N/A
ALASKA		N/A

New LLCs filed

Source of data: International Association of Commercial Administrators (IACA), Annual Reports of the Jurisdictions covering 2001-2005 Missing data bars indicate the data was not reported to IACA for that year.

18

Figure 4

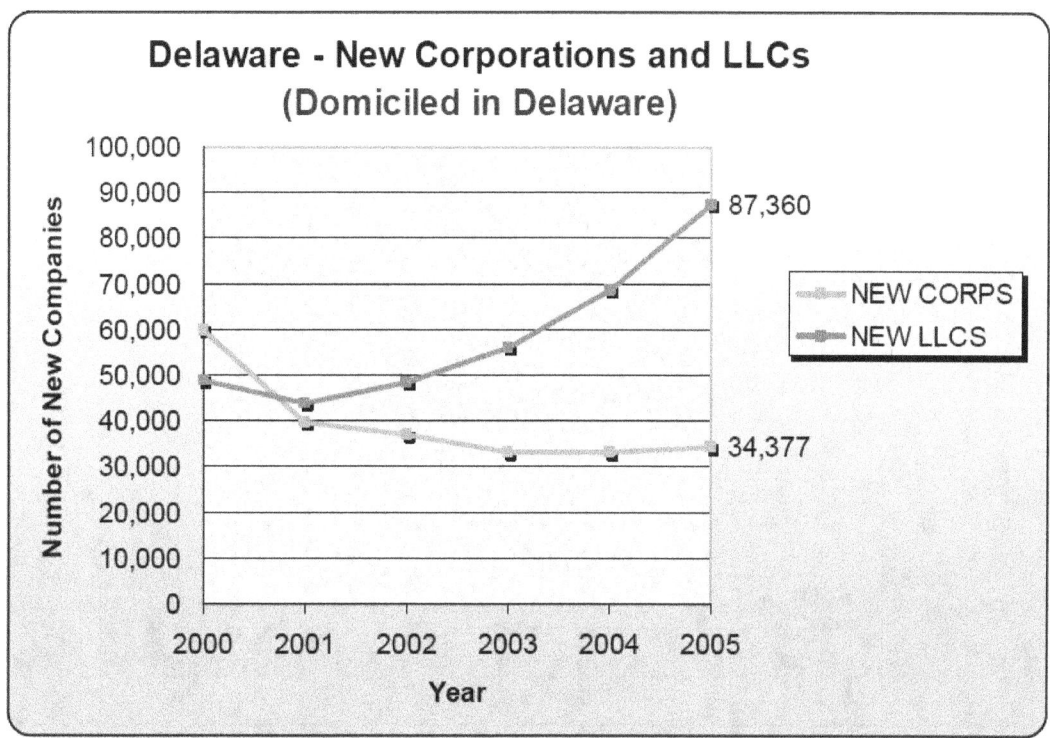

Figure 5

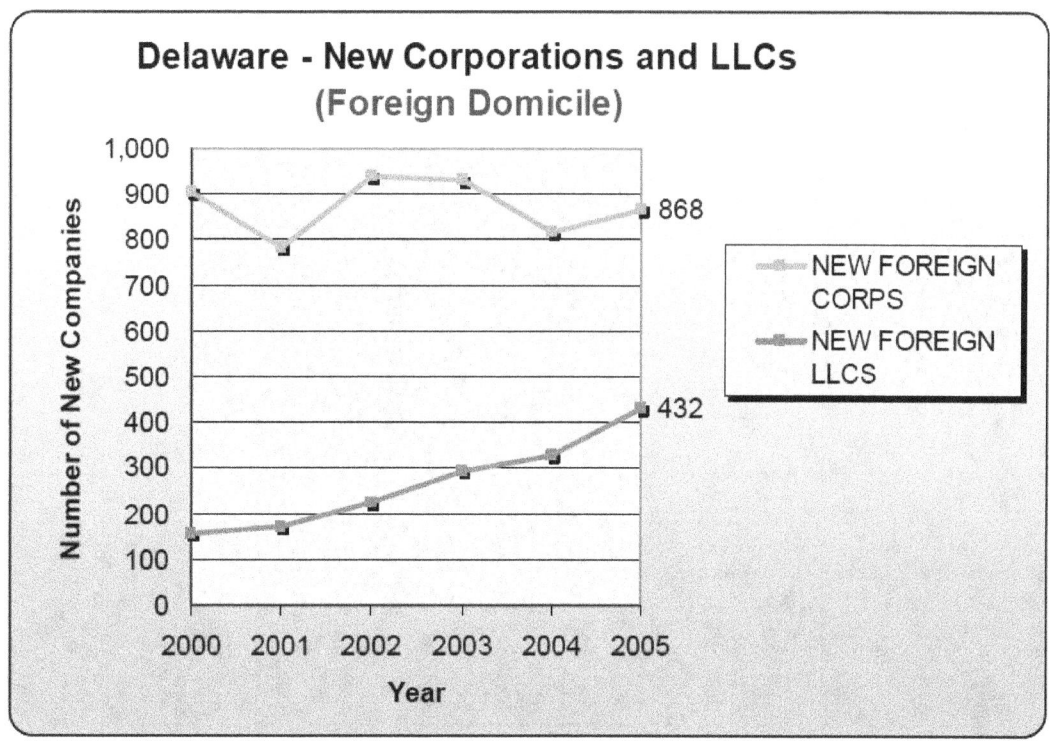

Source of data: Delaware Department of State (2000-2003), IACA Annual Reports of the Jurisdictions (2004-2005)

Figure 6

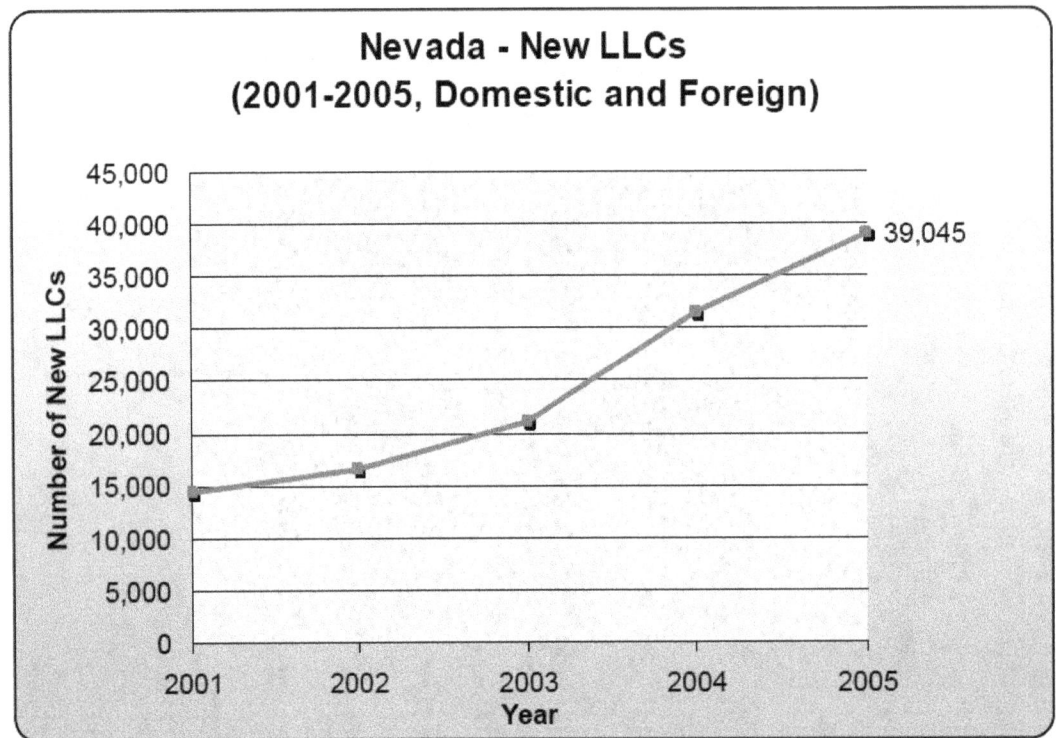

Figure 7

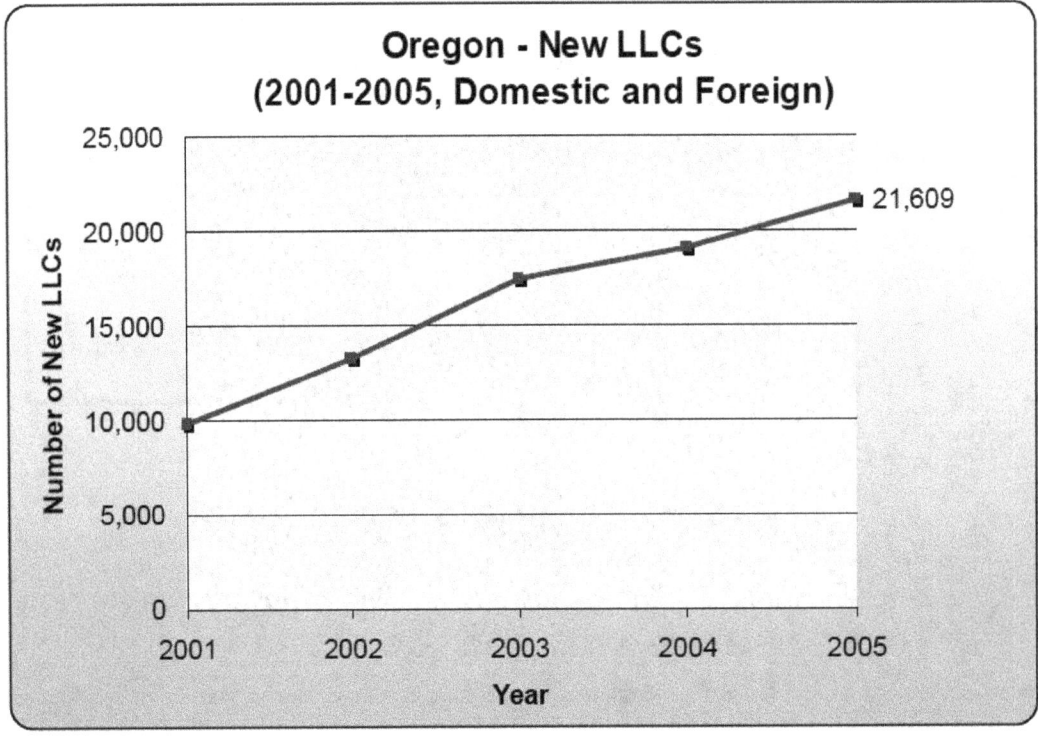

Source of data: IACA Annual Reports of the Jurisdictions, 2003-2006

Figure 8

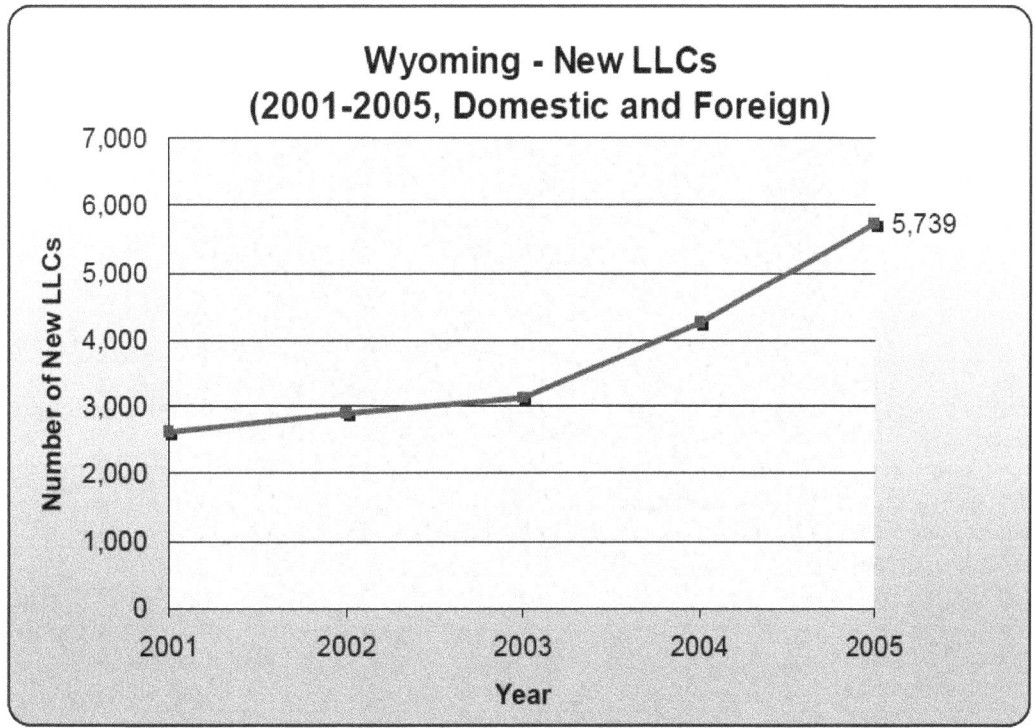

Source of data: IACA Annual Reports of the Jurisdictions, 2003-2006

Table 1 – LLC formation requirements comparison

Requirements:	Delaware	Nevada	Oregon	Wyoming
Number of Organizers	One or more	One or more	One or more	One or more**
Name/Address of Registered Agent/Office	Yes	Yes	Yes	Yes
Name and Address of Members*	No	Yes	Yes***	Yes
Name/Address of Beneficial Owner(s)	No	No	No	No
Cost to File (2005)	$90 ($100 foreign)	$75**** ($75 foreign)	$50 ($50 foreign)	$100 ($100 foreign)

*Management by members is optional. To protect the identity of members, managers can assume management responsibility.

**One person may form the LLC, but it must have two or more members, unless it is a *flexible* LLC, in which a member may assign his/her interest to another person.

***The name of one member or manager is also required for a foreign LLC.

****This fee was lowered from $175 in 2003.

Figure 9

STATE *of* DELAWARE
LIMITED LIABILITY COMPANY
CERTIFICATE *of* FORMATION

- **First:** The name of the limited liability company is _____
  _____

- **Second:** The address of its registered office in the State of Delaware is _____
  _____ in the City of _____ . The
  name of its Registered agent at such address is _____
  _____

- **Third:** (Use this paragraph only if the company is to have a specific effective date of
  dissolution: "The latest date on which the limited liability company is to dissolve is
  _____.")

- **Fourth:** (Insert any other matters the members determine to include herein.)
  _____
  _____
  _____
  _____
  _____
  _____
  _____

In Witness Whereof, the undersigned have executed this Certificate of Formation this
_____ day of _____ , 20_____ .

By:_____
                     Authorized Person(s)

Name:_____
                  Typed or Printed

Figure 10

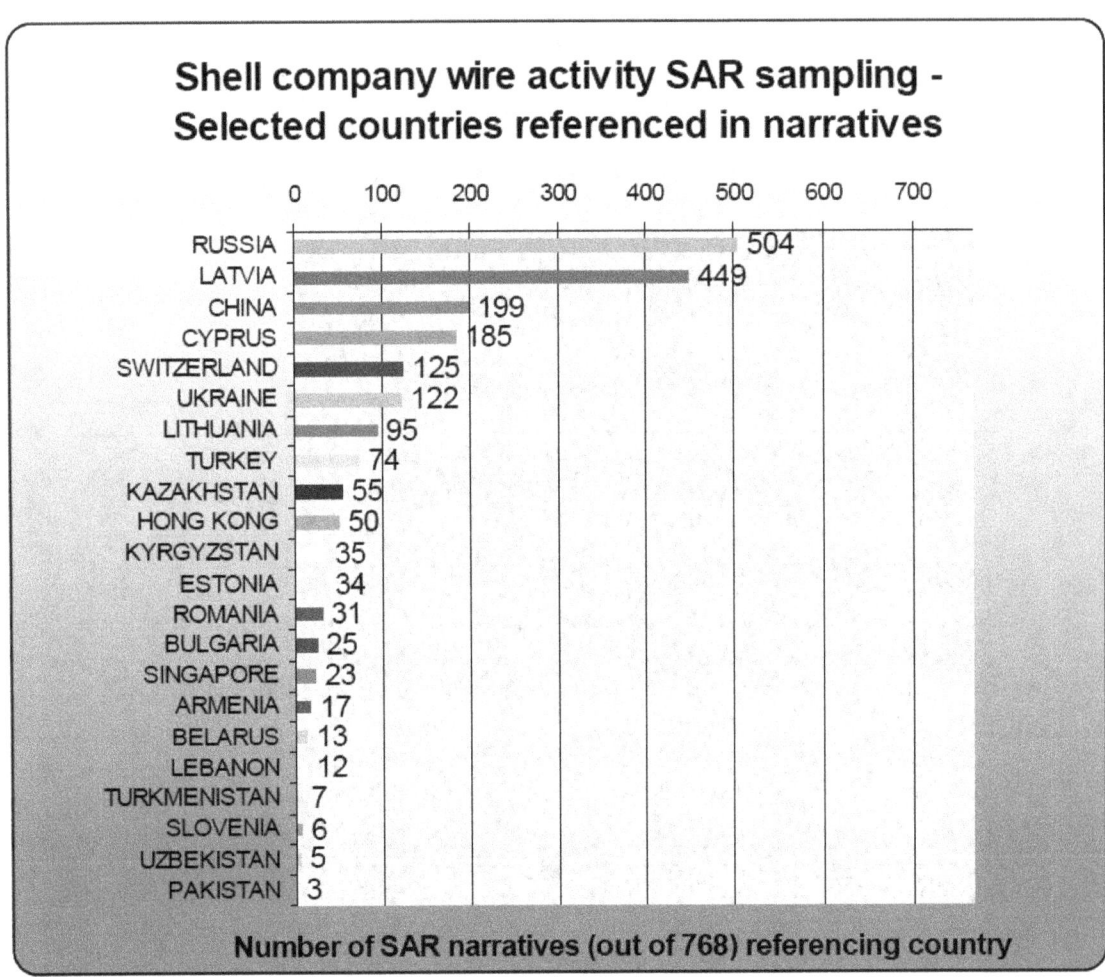

Note the frequency of occurrence for China, Cyprus, and Switzerland, which were often identified in the SARs as destinations of wire transfers from suspected shell companies formed in the United States that had opened accounts in Eastern Europe.

Figure 11

A general model of suspicious wire transfer activity involving domestic shell companies

Wire transfer route →   Alternate wire transfer route ⇢

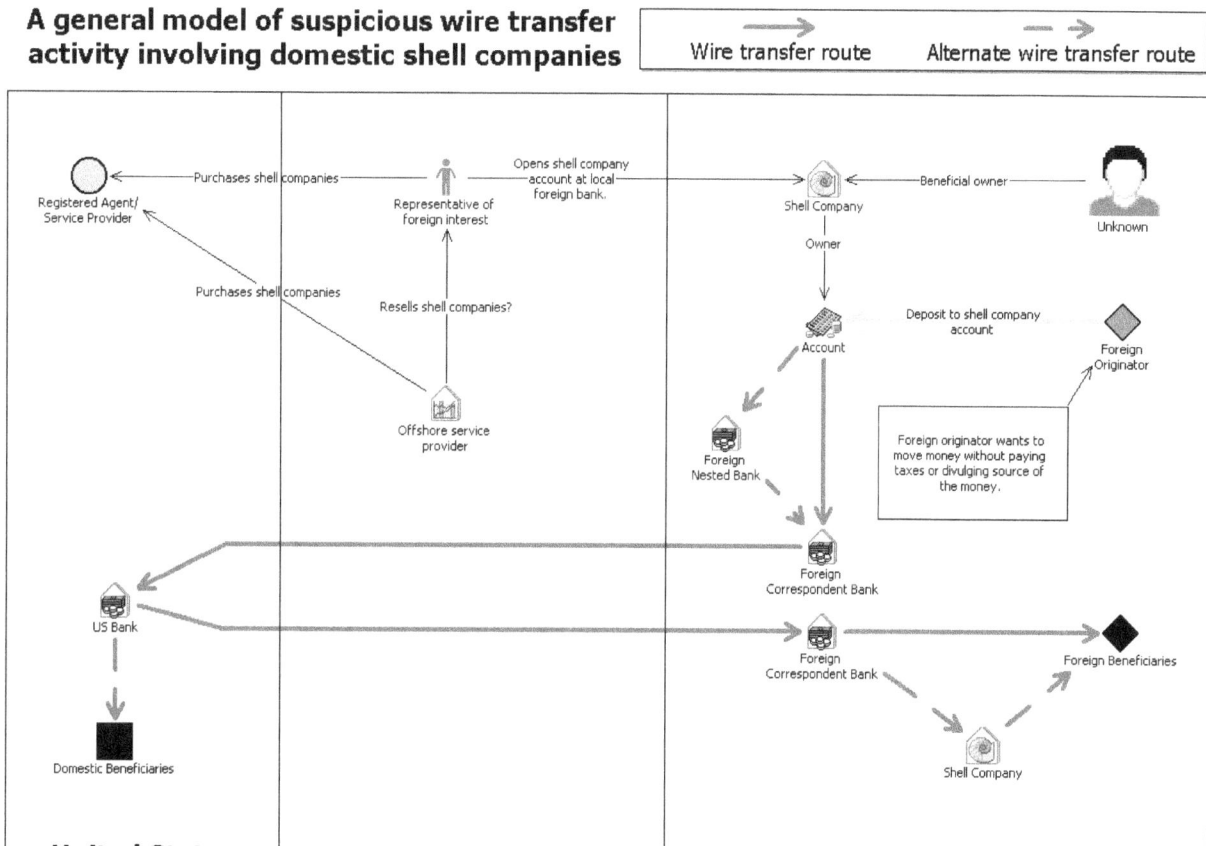

United States

Eastern Europe, Baltics, Cyprus, etc.

The movement of money may vary. However, the flow typically described by the majority of SARs filed on this pattern of activity begins with a foreign account owned by a U.S.-based shell company, often in Russia or Latvia, is sent through the correspondent account of a major U.S. or U.S.-based bank, and goes back overseas to various individual and/or company beneficiaries. The domestic shell company can serve as originator or beneficiary. Additional intermediary banks are often involved.

Figure 12

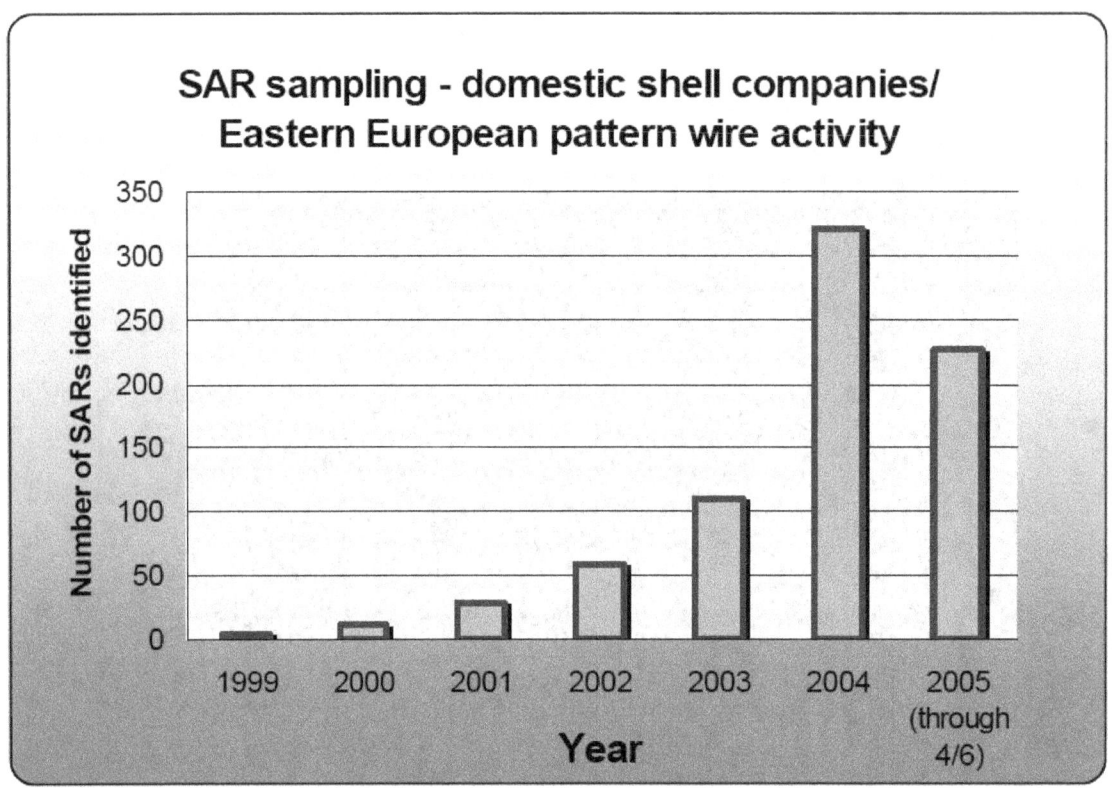

The apparent increase does not necessarily indicate an increase in activity of the magnitude shown, but simply reflects an increase in filing of SARs on this type of activity and the increased ease of identifying activity as being related to domestic shell companies. More likely this is a graphic representation of the lack of reporting in earlier years, as many of the SARs are reviews of past activity filed after the fact. Regulatory and other actions involving ABN Amro Bank, NY and Union Bank of California, for example, have caused those banks to review their records and file more SARs on this activity. These two banks filed 290 of the 768 SARs (37.76%) in the Eastern European/U.S. shell pattern sub-group of the sampling. In addition, a lawsuit filed by a Hong Kong investment group against ABN Amro Bank alleged the bank allowed itself to be used by First Merchant Bank (based in the "Turkish Republic of Northern Cyprus") for money laundering. FinCEN issued a proposed rule regarding First Merchant Bank in August 2004: see http://www.fincen.gov/waisgate1.pdf and http://www.fincen.gov/311fmbextension.pdf.